TWITTER MARKETING STRATEGIES

SMART TIPS ON HOW TO MONETIZE YOUR FOLLOWERS

By Smart Reads

Free Audiobook

As a thank you for being a Smart Reader you can
choose 2 FREE audiobooks from audible.com.
Simply sign up for free by visiting
www.audibletrial.com/Travis to get your books.

Visit:
www.smartreads.co/freebooks
to receive Smart Reads books for FREE

Check us out on Instagram:
www.instagram.com/smart_readers
@smart_readers

ABOUT SMARTREADS

Choose Smart Reads and get smart every time. Smart Reads sorts through all the best content and condenses the most helpful information into easily digestible chunks.

We design our books to be short, easy to read and highly informative. Leaving you with maximum understanding in the least amount of time.

Smart Reads aims to accelerate the spread of quality information so we've taken the copyright off everything we publish and donate our material directly to the public domain. You can read our uncopyright below.

We believe in paying it forward and donate 5% of our net sales to Pencils of Promise to build schools, train teachers and support child education.

To limit our footprint and restore forests around the globe we are planting a tree for every 10 hardcover books we sell.

Thanks for choosing Smart Reads and helping us help the planet.

Sincerely,

Travis & the Smart Reads Team

TABLE OF CONTENTS

INTRODUCTION

You have just added a new and innovative product to your company's portfolio, and you can't wait to tweet about it. The prototype that has been keeping you up all night for the last year is finally done and you are ready to unleash it to the market. You quickly think up some marketing gimmick and your finger instinctively hovers over the button as you prepare yourself to launch it out on Twitter. What goes through your mind? Do you just press the "Send" button and share it with Twittersphere?

This strategy may have worked back in the days when Twitter was still in its nascent stage. Looking at the size of this social media behemoth today, it is likely that your tweet would never get the attention it deserves. It will probably get as much attention as a ripple in a large, serene pond. This may still work if you are targeting a small select group of people, but with the millions of people on Twitter today, you must develop a totally different viewpoint.

You need to consider Twitter as a large pool of information with waves forming and dissipating at different locations and points in time. You may have gone to the beach one bright and sunny day, and before long, your attention is likely to be drawn to the waves breaking on the shoreline. The waves that make it to the shore are the ones that people notice, not the ones that dissipate somewhere in the middle of the sea. The same principle works on Twitter. The tweets that count are those that millions of people notice, so you have to give your tweets more than just a passing thought.

In this book, you will discover the nitty-gritty strategies that will make you a Twitter Marketing master. Are you ready to set the Twittersphere on fire and get your followers clicking and retweeting your tweets? Let's get rolling!

CHAPTER 1: WHY IS TWITTER MARKETING IMPORTANT?

In order to know why Twitter marketing is important, it's important to look at the benefits it offers. Here are ten of those benefits:

1. You can offer unmatched customer service.
How many cases have you heard of or experienced where a customer loses interest in a particular product because the company behind it offered pathetic customer service? It doesn't even matter if the product is superb. As long as you are mistreated when the product breaks down and you require customer service, you will not be happy. Rather than put customers on hold, you should provide real-time answers to the customers needs. Through Twitter, you can provide customers with solutions to their problems right away. On top of that, the Twitter account administrator should be proactive - always searching for online conversations regarding your company so they can provide relevant responses.

2. Your brand will stay current and relevant.
It would be unwise to assume your customers are always thinking about your business. It's easy for them to forget about you and focus on a new industry player. The truth is you must constantly keep your

brand on people's minds, no matter how great your product may be. This is why the biggest companies spend millions on advertising. They recognize the need for brand awareness in order to get customers to keep buying their product. What's more, using Twitter to advertise is free, so why not maximize its use?

3. You can provide interesting, real-time information and establish great relationships.

You can use Twitter for more than just solving your customer's problems or letting them know you still exist. Twitter is also a means to inform them about interesting facts about your products and services. This is a great way to establish relationships with people who aren't your regular customers while maintaining ties to those who are. Over time, you will create brand loyalty as customers view your company as having a human entity rather than a cold, unfeeling corporation. This is a crucial requirement that makes people buy your product and keep them coming back for more.

4. More traffic is driven to your website.

You need to think of your tweets as teasers meant to generate enough buzz to get people to crave more information about your business and its products. There is no other place that can provide better information about your products than your company website. However, driving traffic to the website can be difficult if you can't seduce people in the Twittersphere. So how do you use Twitter to generate enough traffic? Well, there are some surefire strategies that are discussed later in the book. Consider this to be a teaser of things to come, but don't be in a hurry to jump ahead.

5. You get a genuine public perception of your business.

You may enjoy praising your product on the Internet, but you will learn more about what people think of it if you pay attention to what is being said. Be aware that some of the comments will be negative, but this can be a good way of gaining a genuine perspective of how customers perceive the product. You can respond to the negative and positive comments in different ways, but we will reserve this for later sections of the book. It is important you remain cognizant that customers have their own opinion and this can have a tremendous effect on sales. If you don't have a Twitter account, or in touch with the online social media world, you could be basing the popularity of your product on how well the initial sales are going. However, you must realize that this is a marathon and not a sprint, so it is extremely crucial that you maintain a close watch on online public perception.

6. It's easier to track industry trends and competitors.

The truth is that your competitors are also on Twitter, and the size of their following may even scare you. Just remember the number of followers your rivals have shouldn't scare you. Another thing is that competition is healthy for your business and you could steal some of their strategies to increase your sales. Twitter also helps you to stay in touch with local and global trends. You do not want to be considered the outdated company within your industry.

7. Twitter can be used for internal communications

Twitter can be a great way to communicate with employees within your company. It can be used to make sure everyone is aware of what is going on in the company the moment it happens. However, using Twitter for this purpose requires a high level of prudence in order to avoid sharing sensitive information with outsiders. Zappos is a good example of a company that tweets information to employees.

8. You can advertise new products to customers and boost sales.

This may sound obvious as a benefit of Twitter marketing, but most companies underestimate its impact in boosting sales of new products among existing customers. Since most consumers shop on instinct, you will discover the moment you advertise a new product, most of your existing customers will go ahead and buy it without thinking too much about it. Since they already have faith in your current products, a tweet is enough to get them to buy your new offer.

9. Your online brand is enhanced.
If you were to visit the Twitter profile page of any celebrity, you would be amazed at the size of their following. You may not even have half of their followers, but you can still use Twitter to make a huge splash and enhance your reputation. If you increase the number of your followers, your online reputation and credibility will be improved. This will help you sell more products. You will discover how to increase your Twitter followers later on in the book.

10. It helps in management of public relations.
Twitter can be a great way to maximize your public relations. Modern society is made in such a way that a slight mistake by a company can turn into a public relations nightmare. The best way to handle such a situation would be to respond as fast as possible and issue a statement. Wasting time may damage the positive reputation that you've worked so hard to develop. If you wait even one day to respond to a

crisis, you will find your online audience can be very unforgiving.

CHAPTER 2: MASTERING TWITTER MARKETING STRATEGIES

You now know why it is important for you to have a Twitter account for your business, now it's time to discuss the most effective marketing strategies you can use to make sure Twitter draws more customers to your business. Here are the 10 best strategies for your Twitter marketing campaign:

1. Create a Twitter account that will resonate with potential customers.
You must have heard of the saying that "First impressions last," it's actually the same for your project, business or product. In other words, if your Twitter account is lackluster, nobody in the Twittersphere will take you seriously. It is extremely important you do not forget one key aspect of working in the virtual world – just because things are online doesn't mean they aren't real. Your account must have a decent profile photo that sends out a message about your brand in a clear manner. You also have to describe your profile using the 160 characters available, so make sure you pick the right words. Be smart and use hashtags, calls to action, and keywords to prompt customers to take the next step and buy your product. Don't forget to link your company website and add your physical location as well.

2. Establish a segmented Twitter list according to the audience being targeted.

You will not be able to market your product as effectively as possible if you do not know your target audience. Communicating to the wrong target audience is a huge waste of time. It is important you send out your marketing tweets to the right audience. In order to achieve this, you have to use Twitter lists to segment your audience. There is a free Twitter tool known as Followerwonk that can help you look for users whose bios contain similar keywords as your content. There is also the option of searching for users based on their location. Find hashtags that are aligned with your industry and as you browse through them, look for the people who are using them. You can come up with some really great hashtags to use in your marketing strategy. Hootsuite is also another Twitter tool that can help you import your lists, thus making it easier to keep track of the people in your list and establish relationships with them.

3. Maintain a personal relationship with followers by sending direct messages.

Once you have a group of loyal followers, you should make things more personal by sending direct messages to everyone. Since the group is relatively small at first, you can send the messages manually to everyone on your list. However, when the number of followers grow rapidly, it becomes more difficult to do so, and therefore, you need to use a tool such as Social Oomph. This tool sends private messages to all your followers automatically. Whenever someone decides to follow you, they automatically receive a message from you. Make sure that this message is well crafted so that you don't come across as trying to make an overt sales pitch. Just say thank you for their decision to follow you and wish them a great day, or ask them how you may help them. If they respond, then don't forget to include their name in your message. It could be the beginning of a symbiotic relationship where you help them and they help you by promoting your product.

4. Make plans in advance.
There is no need to procrastinate and send out a tweet at the last minute yet you have the opportunity to make plans in advance. A good example is the Christmas period. This is the perfect time to send tweets that will impact your sales considerably, but if you haven't even thought of the tweets you will be sending out, you will end up losing a golden opportunity. Ensure that tweets for every major event are planned in advance. When you send the tweets, don't sit back and disengage; keep the fire burning by being proactive. Follow any related hashtags that

might be trending and use them as a way to engage in marketing. This will help you generate momentum to propel you ahead from your rivals. There is also a powerful tool known as #OwnTheMoment planner that helps monitor upcoming events so you can get the most appropriate tweet relevant for your followers.

5. Utilize Twitter Chats effectively.

Most businesses and businesspeople fail to realize Twitter was designed primarily to enable people to engage with one another. It is not just a tool for promoting your products and services. In other words, if you intend to reap maximum dividends from your marketing campaign, then you must be prepared to engage with your followers actively. Twitter Chats enable you to create a buzz about your product or service, and as you do, people will respond and start talking about what you are offering. You have the choice of either creating your own Twitter chat or looking for a chat relevant to your industry or product. If you decide on the former option, then consider creating cool graphics to get people talking about your product. Just remember that you have to keep participating and engaging constantly with people who respond to your chats. Don't watch from the sidelines. Instead, use @username to make sure they receive notifications every time you send out a reply about the chat.

6. Publicize your events using Promoted Tweets and Promoted Trends.

There are times when all your business requires is a little advertising to draw in more sales. Why don't you use Twitter to get noticed? Promoted Tweets and Promoted Trends are two ways of making a huge splash in ways that conventional online marketing methods can't compete with. The way this works is via retweets, click-throughs, and favorite tweets. The process of buying these Promoted Tweets and Promoted Trends is similar to Google's own model. They are auctioned at a rate relevant to its cost-per-engagement and you pay according to the engagement of the tweet or trend. In order to make the best use of such tools, you should consider using them when you have a major product launch or event. For example, back in 2010, Coke would send out a tweet to celebrate every goal that was scored during the world cup. This generated a lot of engagement. The truth is that most people log in to Twitter just to see the issues that are trending, so by using Promoted Trends and Tweets, you are positioning yourself to take advantage of user curiosity. This kind of advertising can be invaluable.

7. Leverage the power of Twitter Search.
Twitter searches are a great and effective way to find out what is being said about your products and services. For example, if you are running a blog about food, you can use Hootsuite to establish a search about the best chocolate chip recipe. If someone requests for such a recipe on Twitter, you will receive a notification and will be able to respond accordingly. At this stage, you can reply to the person using @username and send them a link to your food blog so they can find the recipe they want. You also have the option of running an advanced search so you discover the people tweeting using a particular keyword within your local area. People will thank you a lot if you can help them get the information they need, and some might even be converted into customers. The point here is not to focus on simply selling a product but rather to provide value to people.

8. Make use of your competitors.
It is likely your rivals are using you on Twitter, so why not return the favor? As long as this is done in an ethical way, everyone benefits. By using the advanced search feature on Twitter, you can look for any hashtags belonging to your competitor and determine who their customers are. The next step is to refine your search so you find those customers who are within any city or country of interest. You should also

consider following your competition so that you stay updated on anything they do. It is inevitable that some of your customers will also be using your rivals' products and services. You can use this opportunity to interact with your competitor's and mutual customers may even join the conversation. Some day you may end up collaborating with the competition on a product or service that will benefit customers immensely, so don't make enemies in business. The relationship may someday become symbiotic!

9. Learn the perfect times to send out tweets.
It is obvious your followers will not be online at all times. This means you have to find out the best tweeting times so your followers will get to see them when they are online. There are a number of tools you can use for this. One of them is SocialBro, which analyzes your followers' timelines and informs you when to tweet. There is also HootSuite, which determines and informs you of the time of day when your tweets usually receive the highest level of engagement. Another tool is Tweriod, which analyzes your followers and informs you whenever they are active online and when you should tweet them. The information you receive regarding the best times to tweet should be imported into the Buffer Schedule. This will help give you the best results possible. These tools will help you know when majority of your

followers are online, and you can then adjust your marketing campaign to send out more tweets during these particular times. At the end of the day, you may not reach everyone, but at least most of your followers will be able to engage with you as you continue building your brand.

10. Engage whenever there are retweets or replies.

Finally, you have to decide what your online persona is going to be like. You must decide whether you are going to watch passively or engage actively with what is happening on Twitter. If you tweet something major, you are likely to be swamped with comments from many of your followers. This may quickly get to your head, but it is important to understand that you should never take for granted the people who follow your brand. One minute they are there, the next minute they have moved on. Every comment must be replied to and every positive tweet that paints your company in a good light should be retweeted for other customers to see. This is part of building your brand. If your products or services are criticized, then you have to take it in stride. You should consider embedding a deep link in your tweets so that whoever has a private message they wish to share with you directly can do so easily. If there is one thing that people are missing today due to all the busyness, it is clear communication. If you are able to take the time and make the effort to communicate more clearly than your competitors, then you will find it much easier to create a bigger impact using Twitter!

CHAPTER 3: 10 BIGGEST TWITTER MARKETING MISTAKES

Making a Twitter marketing campaign a success is always exciting, however, there are potential pitfalls you can still fall into. These are things you must avoid at all costs if you want to ensure your campaign is successful. Let's examine some of the biggest mistakes you can make when it comes to a Twitter marketing campaign, and how to avoid them:

1. Leaving your profile spaces empty.
Maintaining a stellar Twitter profile is important. You must have a good profile photo and well-written description. More importantly, you have to make full use of Twitter by ensuring there are no empty spaces on your profile. The header image must represent the brand you are trying to sell; something that aligns with the image you are trying to project to your customers. If you leave the header image empty, you come across as unprofessional. Take as much time as you need, but make sure you get the best image you can so you can maximize on it.

2. Excessive use of hashtags.
It's understandable you would want to try as much as possible to entice as many people to follow you on Twitter. However, don't fall into the trap of excessively

using hashtags within one sentence. This is going to make you lose followers rather than gain them. What you need to do is to find a few hashtags you can use repeatedly over time. This will prompt your followers to start using the same hashtags in their own tweets, and before you know it, you will be trending!

3. Trying to force connections that aren't there.
Every tweet you put out should flow naturally and in a simple way. Whenever you tweet something, there should be a natural connection that is unforced and likely to be embraced by your followers. On the other hand, if you attempt to force a non-existent connection onto your followers, it is likely to backfire on you. One great example of this is when Pizza Hut launched its Oscars ceremony with the hashtag #AllDressedUpWithPizzaToGo. They requested people who were planning to view the Oscars to send in photos of themselves dressed up and carrying a pizza. This did not resonate with the public as much as Pizza Hut had anticipated, probably because the connection didn't exist or the campaign just sounded ridiculous. The point here is if you want to have influence over your followers, you must focus on real connections. The best way to know this is to use your own gut instinct. You will instinctively know when a campaign is going to be accepted or not.

4. Using the @ symbol to start your tweets.

This is one very common mistake among businesses. They often begin their tweets by using the @ symbol without realizing this is only supposed to be used when you are directly replying to someone. The problem here is that every time you use the @ symbol to tweet something, then the only people who will see it are the person whose name is after the symbol and their followers. Guess who won't see the tweet? Your followers! You will be losing out on a huge opportunity without even knowing it. If you must mention someone specific in a tweet, then you have to place a period at the beginning of the tweet and follow it up with the @ symbol and name of the person. If you do this, Twitter will consider it a regular tweet and your own followers will see the tweet as well. This will enable you to reach a greater number of people that could have been left out.

5. Reusing old tweets all the time.

You may have produced some killer tweets back in the day and so it becomes extremely tempting to just pull one out, dust it off, and recycle it. However, there is a problem when you do this over and over again, reusing old tweets every time just because they were brilliant. If you want to get noticed by the Twittersphere, then the best strategy to use would be to create unique content. If you are unable to come up with anything fresh for your followers, then try to add some unique content to what you had tweeted in the past before sending them out. Maybe you could create an element of uniqueness by adding a photo, or even explain an earlier tweet in greater detail. The aim here is to refresh what worked well for you in the past without boring your followers and appearing unoriginal.

6. Allowing every employee to represent the company brand.

It is often a good idea to encourage every employee in your company to maximize Twitter in order to boost the brand of the company. As long as they put the interests of the company first then everything will be fine. However, there are times when such a policy can backfire on you. This is especially true when you realize you cannot control what your employees are tweeting about when they aren't at work. For example, one of your employees may go ahead and tweet comments and images of just how many beers they downed over the weekend. This may seem irrelevant but can actually hurt the company's reputation. You have to ensure that those people who have been designated to represent the company brand will only use Twitter to make comments that paint the company in a positive light. This is the best way to maintain your good reputation and make sure that your

followers receive the best information about the
company.

7. Protecting your Twitter account.
This is a very silly mistake that may cost you the
opportunity to attract even greater numbers of
followers. Protecting your tweets may seem like a
good idea in the beginning but the problem is that only
the people who follow you will be able to see them. In
other words, the vast majority of people on Twitter
who aren't your followers will never get a chance to
view your tweets. If this happens, they will never
become your followers. By protecting your account, it
also means no one can retweet or favorite your tweets,
which does you a great disservice in terms of getting
the attention the company is looking for.

8. Following everyone you see on Twitter.
If you think that following everyone on Twitter will
boost the chances of him or her following you back,
you are dead wrong. You need to realize there are
many fake and spam accounts on Twitter, so if you
make it a habit to just follow any account without
knowing how they will impact your business, you will
end up disappointed. You should try to focus on
accounts that are likely to give your brand a leg up in
terms of positioning your company where it needs to
be. The connections you form need to be valuable and

useful for learning new information over time. What you need to focus on is creating sustainable relationships with people who will bring value to the company rather than time wasters. As the old saying goes, quality over quantity.

9. Failing to appreciate retweets.
You probably have a lot of people who are always retweeting your content, but have you ever gone to the extent of appreciating them for doing so? It is important for your brand that you return the favor by either thanking them for the retweet or simply retweeting their content. However, you also have to consider the fact that there could be hundreds of people retweeting your comments, thus making it very difficult to thank everyone whenever they do so. The best way to handle this is to make sure you retweet their content once in a while. Whenever you read a tweet that you feel supports the vision your company has or resonates with the type of brand you are trying to build, you should retweet it at once. It is a symbiotic relationship where you and the other person both benefit. On top of that, it can help you build loyalty that may come in handy in the future.

10. Using more than the allotted 140 characters.
Twitter only allows you to send out a tweet that is 140 characters long. Most people think this is barely

enough to get the message across, but the truth is that 140 characters are a lot. You can actually tell people what is on your mind using the 140 characters. The reason why people think they need more characters is because they think their thoughts will not be complete if they try to squeeze them in using only 140 characters. Another issue with trying to squeeze your tweet into 140 characters is you might be forced to break a few grammatical rules along the way, which is something your brand does not want to be associated with. If you make the effort to use the 140 characters available, you will realize that with a bit more practice, it is possible to say everything you need to say and still be understood. Besides, people prefer smaller chunks of information, so that one tweet may be enough to effectively get your message across.

CHAPTER 4: TOP 10 DO'S OF A WINNING TWITTER CAMPAIGN

In the previous chapter, we looked at the things that you should not do if you want your marketing campaign to be successful on Twitter. In this chapter, we are going to discuss some of the things that you need to do to get the best results from your marketing strategies. If you are looking for ways of adding more bite to your campaign, then the following 10 principles are going to help propel you in the right direction.

1. Do maintain a constant presence on Twitter.
In other words, make sure you are tweeting as much as possible. Remember how we described the Twittersphere as a vast sea you can easily get lost in if you are unable to make a big enough ripple? Well, that is exactly what is likely to happen if you do not tweet on a regular basis. It is the best way to ensure your followers and others feel your presence. You don't have to go crazy and send out a tweet every hour. It could be just a few or maybe one tweet a day. This should be enough to let the Twitterati know you are still alive. What you need to realize is that people on Twitter have a very short memory. If you do not make the conscious decision to maintain a constant presence on Twitter, then you will fade very quickly from the consciousness of the Twitterati. You need to

tweet regularly in order to impose yourself on people's minds. It may seem like a chore but it actually doesn't even require much time and effort to post a few tweets every day. However, do not go for quantity over quality, so make sure every tweet is worth it so you receive the positive recognition you desire.

2. Do schedule your tweets properly.
In order for a marketing strategy to be effective, it must be well planned. This principle can also be applied to tweeting. When you sit down and create a plan of how you are going to schedule your tweets, you will discover that achieving great results isn't difficult. On top of that, the schedule will help you stay constant in the regularity of your tweets such that you will not forget to tweet on any given day. For example, you may plan your tweets one month ahead of schedule. You have to be careful, however, about scheduling tweets for upcoming events since these may end up being canceled abruptly. This is likely to leave you with a number of tweets about an event that didn't even take place, resulting in embarrassment.

3. Do follow people with a specific plan in mind.
One of the don'ts discussed in the last chapter had to do with following everyone in Twitter just to boost your follower count. On the other hand, you should also avoid following big influencers who have a

massive following, even though you may be in the same industry. What you need to understand is that these influencers may be able to teach you a lot from their comments and tweets, and they may even somehow help you grow your following, but it will be very difficult for you to engage in a conversation with them. You need to hook up with people who are genuinely willing and able to engage with you on a regular basis so you can share ideas and information. Try to find people whom you sense can be of benefit, even if they do not have many followers.

4. Do take advantage of videos as a way of telling stories.
It is possible that you are a creative genius who can come up with amazing tweets. You could be an awesome wordsmith who knows how to spin a tale using words or perhaps you are great at using images to get your message across. However, do you know the power that a video message contains? Yes, it is not possible to send out every single tweet with a video embedded into it, but if you have a burning message to deliver to your followers, then a video can be a great tool to do just that. The truth is that in today's world, video has a lot of power among the masses, so if you want to improve your engagement with people, you can't go wrong with video. The best aspect of using video is that the information being conveyed tends to

stick in the minds of people for a longer period of time. The combination of audio and visual messages provides a compelling and effective tool for helping people retain a particular message. In fact, making a video is not really that difficult, and you could even have one professionally made.

5. Do inform people about your promotions.
There are a huge number of people who have Twitter accounts just so they can stay informed about the latest promotion or special offer. It would be unfortunate for your company if you did not meet their demand for such information. If you fail to put out information about any of your promotions or offers, these potential customers will switch their allegiance to a different brand, assuming they were loyal to you in the first place. Everybody appreciates a discount or free item once in a while, so it is important you take this into account when you are trying to market your brand over the Internet.

Obviously, this promotion or special offer will not be a perpetual situation, and ultimately, you will discover that you have gained many new customers. You will also have made the relationship with your current customers stronger.

6. Do make yourself easy to find.
From what we have discussed in the previous sections, having a great Twitter profile is one of the best ways of ensuring you create the right influence. It will help you garner people's attention and get them clicking on your tweets and links. On the other hand, there are a lot of people who may not know you exist and are looking for a company just like yours. With Twitter being such a big place, how will they even find you? The first thing you have to do is make sure the name associated with your Twitter account bears a resemblance to the name of your business. You should also make sure the right keywords are part of your profile so that customers looking for products can find you easily. It would be a great shame if you worked on creating the perfect profile only to realize nobody is reading it because you are so hard to find!

7. Do remember to adhere to the Golden Ratio when posting content on Social Media.
If you spend all your time posting content that talks about your business every single time, you will lose a lot of followers in a short period of time. It is important you remember to stick to the rule, which defines the ratio of how you should distribute your content – 30% of it should be owned, 60% of it should be curated, and the remaining 10% should be promotional. If you follow this ratio, you will discover

it is easier to develop a loyal following over time. This strategy will help you avoid being perceived as one of those companies always looking for an opportunity to shove their products down the throats of customers. You will be viewed as a business interested in providing genuine value to people's lives, and your followers will be glad they are following you.

8. Do make use of Tweet Chats.
If you want to stay updated on what is going on within your industry, then you should use Tweet Chats. These are scheduled and regulated chats held between members of a Twitter group. You will be able to keep track of the latest news and engage with other people, with the end result being a substantial increase in your Twitter following. This is a great way to network with others in a fun and informal setting. You will get to meet new people, learn from them, and even help them out in return. The connections you make may serve you well for a very long time; so make sure to use Twitter Chats for your benefit.

9. Do keep your links short.
When you are in the process of working on your marketing campaign, you will find yourself constantly posting tweets with links to interesting content. However, you need to be careful you do not post links that are extremely long, confusing, and hard to read. If

the link is too long, the person reading it won't be able to tell what the name on the link says. You must shorten your links, and the best way to this is to use bit.ly. This is an account that will reduce the length of your links every time you need to post, thus improving the viewing experience of the audience you are targeting. The best part of it all is that using bit.ly is absolutely free.

10. Do be sincere.

You may have decided you are not going to get desperate in your attempts to sell your products or services to people, and that's commendable. However, on occasions that you do decide to pitch your product to the market, you should always be sincere about it. Let's look at M&M's marketing campaign for the Oscars. They created a fake movie trailer and even informed the public it was just a mock video. In the process, they were honest enough to request people to consume more of their products.

The promotional video had a YouTube release a couple of days prior to the Oscars, and what was realized was that it was much more entertaining and useful than all the tweets that M&M's sent out during the awards week. The lesson to be learned here is that as a company, you need to be sincere whenever you are promoting your products and services to the public. There is no reason to pretend like you don't have motives of pushing your products when it is clear for everyone to see. This will allow you to create a bigger impression on people's minds.

CHAPTER 5: BONUS TIPS TO TURN YOUR MARKETING INTO A SUCCESS

By using these tips, you will add an extra boost to your Twitter marketing campaign. Doing these right will help you achieve the dizzying heights of success most people only dream about.

Tip 1: Include keywords in every tweet.
It's important to add keywords in every tweet you send out. This is the best way to ensure that people find your tweets and they have the desired impact. Find keywords relevant to whatever industry you are in and use them in your tweets. Make sure the keywords describe the business you are in and can propel you forward in your marketing campaign.

Tip 2: Learn how to retweet properly in order to gain attention.
When most people think about retweeting someone else's comments, they simply press the retweet button. It seems to be the best and easiest thing to do, right? However, what you are doing is making it much harder for the original commenter to thank you for retweeting them. What happens is that they will receive a notification informing them you have retweeted them, yet they will be unable to appreciate you for your retweet because that option isn't

available from the notification panel. The best thing to do when retweeting someone's comments is to copy and paste the tweet into your tweet box, add RT before the tweet, and then send. You can also choose to modify someone's tweet by adding MT (modified tweet) before the tweet. These two steps will show people, including the original commenter, that the tweet you have sent is not your own and has been modified. TweetDeck is also another tool you can use to edit and share tweets. It also alerts the original commenter about your retweet and enables them to respond easily, thus saving them the time and trouble of having to search for your retweet manually.

Tip 3: Apply hashtags properly.
The importance of hashtags in Twitter cannot be stressed enough. Everyone knows that using hashtags when tweeting is one of the best ways to get yourself noticed, so finding the best hashtags to associate with is paramount for any marketing campaign. One tool that you can make use of is Hashtagify. This tool allows you to look for any hashtag you feel might serve your marketing campaign well. All you have to do is type in the hashtag of your choice into the Search box and then press Enter. This will generate a list of every popular hashtag somehow related to what you had in mind. When you click on the button Table Mode, you will be able to view the list of hashtags in

order of popularity. This will help you decide which ones to use. Alternatively, you can decide to use Rite Tag, a tool that allows you to check how relevant your hashtag of choice is. To use Rite Tag, sign in and then type the hashtag within your Compose box. You will see your hashtag displayed in a certain color that indicates the rating of the hashtag. Red symbolizes that the hashtag has been overused, blue means it is a cool hashtag, and green signifies that it is good.

Tip 4: Generate content ideas from the right places.

You may be overflowing with content ideas you want to use on Twitter. If that's true, then great! On the other hand, you may be drawing blanks in terms of new ideas. So then, where can you find fresh ideas for your content? Why don't you try Twitter itself? Just type in the keywords relevant to the industry you are in and check out what people are saying out there. This will help you get a feel for the market within your specific business niche and will provide you with fresh insight about the things you should be focusing on when tweeting. Another thing is that you must keep tabs on the content being shared by your followers. In most cases, their content could be related to the things that you want to comment about. You will discover they are frequently asking questions that aren't being answered by anyone out there. This is your opportunity to step in and fill that gap. Send out a tweet that answers their question and clarifies the issues they are concerned with. If you follow this approach, you will discover that you always have a lot of information to use to formulate your tweets.

Tip 5: Use lead generation cards.
Ultimately, your goal is to convert that follower into a loyal paying customer, right? It is one thing to entice people to go to your website landing page but there is more that you can do to close that deal. You should consider going as far as encouraging people to join your mailing list by using a lead generation card. These cards are available on Twitter and allow you to acquire the emails and Twitter handles of anyone who clicks on the card. You can also keep it simple by sending out tweets asking people to sign up to the company's mailing list. However, the card approach is easier since there are no hassles setting it up and you can use great visuals to draw people's interest.

Tip 6: Introduce yourself personally to your followers by engaging with their tweets.
The fact that there are thousands of followers following your account makes it very difficult to engage with every single one of them. However, this doesn't mean you shouldn't take the time to show some interest in the things that they tweet about. By

making the effort to engage with your followers, you will be able to communicate your message in a powerful way that garners the attention you need. Don't just use Twitter to promote yourself. Read what other influencers have written and then send them a direct message telling them your thoughts on their post. This is actually a better approach than simply retweeting what someone has posted because it provides a more enhanced level of interaction. People will start to notice you more and more, and before long, the number of people following you will increase greatly!

Tip 7: Use the Favorite function but avoid overdoing it.

Favoriting the tweets sent out by other people is one of the most effective ways to get yourself noticed. On the other hand, it is important to be careful in the way that you go about doing this. Twitter can suspend your account if they determine that you are excessively favoriting the tweets of others. Such kind of aggressive use of the favorite function is a no-no and frowned upon. What you need to do is find tweets that genuinely merit a favorite. You should also avoid auto-favoriting tweets because every single tweet that mentions your name will also end up being favorited. The problem with this is that you might end up accidentally favoriting a tweet about a tragic murder in a family, thus causing yourself huge embarrassment. The fact that your profile contains all the tweets you have favorited should be reason enough to be prudent in how you use this function.

Tip 8: Leverage the power of images.
You can make your tweets much more effective by using videos but you should also consider incorporating images into your tweets as well. It has been proven that tweets that have images tend to attract a greater level of interest and engagement than those that do not have them. Make use of Twitshot, a web-based tool that enables you to find the most relevant images to use for the links shared in your tweets. This online tool works with any browser, and what you need to do is simply write your tweet, paste the link, and use Twitshot to get images that match your link. If you already have your own photos then you can go ahead and use them, but Twitshot provides you with a greater variety of options. You should remember to always practice prudent use of images. You don't have to use them all the time. You can alternate between images, videos, and not attaching anything at all.

Tip 9: Arouse people's natural curiosity.
Human beings are naturally curious. They want to know what makes certain things tick. You should try

to use this curiosity to your advantage such that whenever you post a backlink to your website, you have already figured out how to entice people to pay attention to your message. Think of ways of tapping into people's curious nature. Your aim should be to arouse people's interest in whatever you are promoting. For example, if you penned a post about how to manage stress, and you want people to click the link and read the article, you should come up with an attractive tagline. A good example would be "Stress management: What you didn't know," rather than "Stress management: What you may prefer to know." You can see the difference between the two taglines, where one compels people to read the post while the other simply makes a suggestion.

Tip 10: Recommend, share, and request people to share your content.
One of the best things about Twitter is that everyone can work together to benefit from the platform. You can decide to share the content that other people tweet about and even recommend their products to influential people you know. It is likely that when you do someone a favor like this, they will also do the same for you. However, there are times when people do not reciprocate such favors. Why? Simply because you haven't asked them to do so! The truth is that people are often ready and willing to recommend you

and share your content with others if you take the time to ask for their help. There are also many people in the Twittersphere who are ready to offer their assistance even though they have never received your help in the first place. If you want to get people to share your content, then you have to take the first step and do them a favor!

Tip 11: Develop your own unique voice and passion.

If you have any intention of standing out of the crowd on Twitter, then you must make the decision to develop your own unique voice. But how do you go about acquiring this unique voice? The best way to develop your voice is to find your passion and follow it. The problem with most of us is that we try to be good at everything and begin to dabble in things that are not in our scope of focus. When we realize that people are getting bored despite our best attempts to produce great content, we begin to wonder what's going wrong. People are interested in seeing content that is relevant to your brand image. In other words, what you represent as an individual or company is exactly what people expect you to focus on. This is the reason why they even bother to follow you at all! People expect that you will be posting stuff that matches what you stand for. If you can stick to what you are passionate about, then people will see this burning desire in your tweets and will stay loyal to you.

Tip 12: Use Promoted Tweets to target a specific audience.

While there is usually emphasis placed on the content of the messages sent out on Twitter, it's important to realize that there should be a focus on the target of that message. Promoted tweets can be extremely useful when creating a marketing campaign, but they are also very effective when targeting a select group of people. They allow you to send messages to specific audiences rather than all your followers. To use this function, just choose Promoted Only when creating your tweet, and send it to the target group. The rest of your followers will not see the tweet, and this may be beneficial in cases where the message is already well known to them. You should keep in mind that promoted tweets do not appear in your timeline but can be found via conducting a search.

Tip 13: Have your tweets embedded into your website or blog.

There is no need to take screenshots of your tweets and place them on your blog. Simply embed your preferred tweets into your website so anyone who goes to your website will be able to scroll through the tweets as if they are seeing them on Twitter. This will enhance the chances of spreading your tweets to a greater number of people. This method is extremely simple yet at the same time, very effective.

Tip 14: Take every opportunity to build credibility.

It is critical for your marketing campaign that you build the credibility you need to be taken seriously. This involves admitting whenever you are wrong and agreeing to improve on those business aspects that require improvement. There are people who will point out your mistakes and attempt to correct you, so always try to keep an open mind and take criticism in your stride.

Examine what people are saying critically and look at the intent of the source of the criticism. If they are right, then acknowledge their input and make the necessary adjustments. In the same vein, if you do make a blunder, avoid the temptation to cover it up regardless of its size. People respect honesty and appreciate it whenever someone confesses their mistake and take steps to put things right. It shows people that you do not allow your ego to control you. You should also avoid overpromising and under delivering as this will lead to loss of the credibility that you have struggled to build over time.

Tip 15: Monitor the performance of your tweets.
There was a time when the only means of tracking the performance of your tweet was to use 3rd party tools or pay for Twitter ads. However, times have changed and today, you can easily access such information inside Twitter itself. The irony is that you still need to register with Twitter ads so that you can access the Twitter Analytics feature. The good thing is that you do not have to buy any ads to use the feature. Just sign up using the name of your business, credit card, and email address. Don't worry about being charged for anything – this can only happen if you decide to actually buy an ad. Twitter analytics allows you to view information such as how many times your links have been clicked, the number of retweets you have, as well as replies. You will also be able to determine the most appropriate times to send tweets and how to word them so that you get the best responses. All this is absolutely free so make sure that you take maximum advantage of Twitter analytics.

Tip 16: Use Twitter's Influencer lists.
One effective way to squeeze out maximum value from your marketing campaign is to make use of Twitter's influencer lists. You have the option of creating your very own influencer list or you can find existing ones to use. To find these existing lists, use the Twitter search feature and pick the lists that are most relevant

for your business. You can even search for any interesting content posted by these influencers by using the mobile app from HootSuite. You will be able to share this content with your followers and in the process, provide them with valuable content. Using influencer lists is actually a good way of following several people at the same time instead of having to find individuals one by one, which can be a long process. There are so many lists to choose from, and you should take it slowly when going through them so that you end up with a list of people who will add value to you and your business.

Tip 17: Post Instagram photos using IFTTT.
If you tend to use a lot of images in your tweets, then you need to know that you can use Instagram to post photos in your timeline. However, the Instagram images tend to appear as links and this simply won't do for your marketing strategy. The solution is to use If This, Then That (IFTTT) if you want your Instagram photos to appear as full images for your followers to view.

Tip 18: Mobilize community support in brand building.
Getting the support of your community is one way of moving people to engage with your brand. Take that first step and ask your followers to offer suggestions

on ways of improving things. You will be pleasantly surprised to see how people respond to such requests. A good example of mobilizing community support is when planning the launch of a prototype. You may require help in coming up with a slogan for the new product, and using your audience for inspiration can be a great way to solve the problem. They can provide some useful ideas that you can then use to overcome your writer's block. Ultimately, you both win because your audience also feels valued by your request for assistance.

Tip 19: Provide discounts and special offers.
People are always on the lookout for discounts and special offers from businesses. If you are not already providing such deals for your followers, then it is time that you started. These deals are what attract customers to buy products from one company over those of another, and you do not want to be left behind. For example, you can create a competition where the first 100 people to retweet your post will receive one of your products at half price. This should not be considered an expense but rather a marketing strategy that draws in more people than would normally be interested in the product. You can also offer free samples to entice more customers and create a bigger loyal following. Everyone will be

keeping track of your Twitter account just in case they can benefit from such deals.

Tip 20: Synchronize your LinkedIn account with Twitter.

If you have not yet opened a LinkedIn account, it is very important that you do so as soon as possible. Then you need to sync it with your account on Twitter so that you can reap maximum benefits whenever you share content on either one of these platforms. Another benefit is that you will be able to monitor other professionals on LinkedIn who are sending out tweets. The first step in the entire process of syncing your accounts is to add the Twitter account to the LinkedIn account. This will give people on LinkedIn a chance to view your profile on Twitter easily. The next step is to install the application LinkedIn Tweets in your LinkedIn profile. This will let you see just how many of your LinkedIn connections have Twitter accounts. To make it much easier to access tweets from your LinkedIn connections, make a Twitter list of everyone who has accounts on both platforms. Syncing your accounts allows you to keep track of any tweets or posts written by important business connections.

CONCLUSION

Throughout this book, you have studied some of the best strategies that you can use today to create and master a successful marketing campaign on Twitter. The information you have learned is useful and will serve you well if you decide to put them into practice the right way.

These strategies are effective in setting you on the right path towards marketing your product or service on Twitter. The introductory chapter was just a taste of things to come, and for sure, you have learned many of the benefits that come with using Twitter to boost your company brand. You found out a number of things that you need to do and also those that you must avoid if you intend on reaping maximum results from your Twitter campaign. There were also numerous tips described in the book.

If you utilize the information, you will have taken a giant leap toward mastering Twitter for your marketing needs. All you need to focus on is making that big splash and generating huge waves that will get you attention and followers. Is there a better time to begin making those waves than now? It's time to take your company brand to the next level, and beyond!

THANKS FOR READING

We really hope you enjoyed this book. If you found this material helpful feel free to share it with friends. You can also help others find it by leaving a review where you purchased the book. Your feedback will help us continue to write books you love.

The Smart Reads library is growing by the day! Make sure and check out the other wonderful books in our catalog. We would love to hear which books are your favorite.

Visit:
www.smartreads.co/freebooks
to receive Smart Reads books for FREE

Check us out on Instagram:
www.instagram.com/smart_readers
@smart_readers

Don't forget your 2 FREE audiobooks.
Use this link www.audibletrial.com/Travis to claim
your 2 FREE Books.

SMART READS ORIGINS

Smart Reads was born out of the desire to find the best information fast without having to wade through the sheer volume of fluff available online. Smart Reads combs through massive amounts of knowledge compiles the best into quick to read books on a variety of subjects.

We consider ourselves Smart Readers, not dummies. We know reading is smart. We're self taught. We like to learn a TON about a WIDE variety of topics. We have developed a love for books and we find intelligence attractive.

We found that each new topic we tried to learn about started with the challenge of finding the pieces of the puzzle that mattered most. It becomes a treasure hunt rather than an education.

Smart Reads wants to find the best of the best information for you. To condense it into a package that you can consume in an hour or less. So you can read more books about more topics in less time.

OUR MISSION

Smart Reads aims to accelerate the availability of useful information and will publish a high quality book on every major topic on amazon.

Smart Reads hopes to remove barriers to sharing by taking the copyright off everything we publish and donating it to the public domain. We hope other publishers and authors will follow our example.

Our goal is to donate $1,000,000 or more by 2020 to build over 2,000 schools by giving 5% of our net profit to Pencils of Promise.

We want to restore forests around the globe by planting a tree for every 10 physical books we sell and hope to plant over 100,000 trees by 2020.

Doesn't it feel good knowing that by educating yourself you are helping the world be a better place? We think so too...

Thanks for helping us help the world. You Smart Reader you...

Travis and the Smart Reads Team

WHY I STARTED SMART READS

Every time I wanted to learn about something new I'd have to buy 20 books on the topic and spend way too long sorting through them and reading them all until I arrived at the big picture. Until I had enough perspectives to know who was just guessing, who was uninformed and who had stumbled upon something remarkable.

I wished someone else could just go in and figure that out for me and tell me what matters. That's how smart reads was born. I want smart reads to be a company that does all that research up front. Sorts through all the content that is available on each topic and pulls out the most up to date complete understanding, then have people smarter than me package the best wisdom in an easy to understand way in the least amount of words possible.

For example, I got a new puppy so I wanted to learn about dog training. I bought 14 different books about dog training and by the time I got through the first 5 and finally started getting the big picture on the best way to train my puppy she had grown up into a dog.

Yeah she's well behaved. She doesn't poop in the house. I can get her to sit and come when I call. But what if someone else went in and read all those books for me, found the underlying themes and picked out the best information that would give me the big picture and get me right to the point. And I'd only have to read one book instead of 15.

That would be amazing. I would save time. And maybe my dog would be rolling over, cleaning up after my kids and doing the dishes by now. That my friend, is the reason I started smart reads. Because I wanted a company I can trust to deliver me the best information in an easy to understand way that I can digest in under an hour. Because dog training is one of many subjects I want to master.

The quicker I can learn a wide variety of topics the sooner that information can begin playing a role in shaping my future. And none of us knows how long that future will be. So why not do everything we can to make the best of it and consume a ton of knowledge. And I figured all the better if I can also make a positive difference in the world.

That's why we're also building schools, planting trees and challenging ideas about copyright's place in today's world. Because as a company we have to be doing everything we can to support the ecosystem that gives us all these beautiful places to read our books. Thanks for reading.

Travis

Customers Who Bought This
Customers Who Bought This Book
Also Bought

Understanding Affiliate Marketing: An Internet Marketing Guide for How To Make Money Online Using Products, Websites and Services

Passive Income: Do What You Want When You Want and Make Money While You Sleep

Blockchain Revolution: Understanding the Internet of Money

The Everything Store Sales Guide: How to Make Money with Amazon FBA

A Detailed Guide in Building A Successful Photography Business Online: Learn How to Market, Sell, Promote and Make Money as a Photographer

Overcoming Procrastination: Proven Strategies on How To Improve Focus, Get Things Done and Achieve Your Goals

Develop Self-Discipline: Daily Habit to Make Self Confidence and Will Power Automatic

Artificial Intelligence: Understanding A.I. and the Implications of Machine Learning